Who Holds The Cards Now?

5 Lethal Steps
to Win His Heart
and Get Him to Commit

By Gregg Michaelsen

Who Holds the Cards Now?
5 Lethal Steps to Win His Heart and Get Him to Connect

By Gregg Michaelsen
"Confidence Builder"

Copyright © 2013 Gregg Michaelsen

ISBN-13: 978-0615902364
ISBN-10: 0615902367

CONTENTS

INTRODUCTION

I'm truly excited about this book, *Who Holds the Cards Now?*

It's time for a pro, a man that may have been able to manipulate you in the past to chime in and help you out. I've read the girl books helping girls and to be honest some are pretty good. But many are written by obvious man haters that think all guys suck.

If you want to turn the tables on men listen to a **man**.

My advice applies to all women in a relationship or seeking a man. You're 18 and just starting college. You're married with three kids. You're 22 and into the bar scene. You're a virgin. You're hot, overweight, average, shy or ugly. I don't CARE!

The only time my advice does not apply is if you are an older couple. The "game" does not need to be played because you have found your way... And I bow to you.

To be honest, many guys **do** suck—but do you know why? Because **you** allow them to. It's a perpetual system: guys go out and women are on edge. We change into roles that we think you are going to like. Call it manipulation or lies but we feel we need to exaggerate who we are or how much money we make just to get your attention, let alone get into your pants. Yes we are assholes when we are wearing our capes on Friday nights but why? Because **you** just got burned two weeks earlier and you are in NO mood to welcome us into your heart.

You are NOT meeting the true us. You are meeting some ugly version of us that to survive needs to become something we are not.

I'm not blaming you. I'm not blaming us. I'm explaining in blunt terms how it is!

These are the cards that I will deal to you.

I'm going to teach you things that you never knew in this book. You will be the boss. You will decide who you will date and when. You will be the one breaking up and **only** if **you** want to. You will never be emotionally manipulated by a man again. Saturday nights you will **always** have a date. Marriage? That will be your choice. Got a couch potato? GONE! He's getting overweight? Guess what, he's now going to the gym!

I am going to give you the Kryptonite that will seduce men.

The bottom line: you will be able to neutralize any man, including myself, a feat that is by no means easy. And you know what? I want you to. Do you think I like the game of driving to the hoop? I don't.

Who am I and why am I qualified to give you advice? I make a living on the other side. I teach men all about you ladies. I can tell you exactly how you come across to men and EXACTLY what you do wrong because I am the guy trying to pick you up. I have a sound understanding of the dynamics of interpersonal relationships.

These two books are all you need, please read them both:

Who Holds the Cards Now? is a must-read for women who are in relationships. This book will also help the single woman understand and find the right man.

The Social Tigress is a must-read for single women. We build your confidence, define who you are and get you out there to find that great guy.

You are going to learn things about men that you **never** knew before. I will show you exactly how to get your man to **desire** you again or for the first time.

I will tell you **exactly** what you are doing wrong and I will give you the solution. If you execute my advice you **will** change your dating life. If you continue to take the same road you're on, you will go nowhere. One of my biggest problems isn't getting women to believe my solutions; rather, the problem comes from getting them to execute my five steps.

Please do not feel insulted. I am trying to convey facts to you like a guy does to another guy for a reason. If you want to learn how to hook us, then you need to know how we think. Guys are blunt; I am going to be the same with you.

IF YOU CHANGE, YOU WILL KEEP HIM – IF YOU DON'T, HE WILL LOSE YOU

Repeat above.

Who Holds the Cards Now?

5 LETHAL STEPS TO WIN HIS HEART & GET HIM TO COMMIT

This is a shocking report made so simple that you may need to sit down. No bull, just five steps to get him off his lazy ass and realize the quality of what he has lying right under him...YOU!

I will tell what you're doing wrong right now and then you and I are going to change your man with five **devastating** tactics. If you're seeking a boyfriend then this book will help you get the guy. At the end of my report I will give you tips and tricks to sustain your relationship as long as you want, and on your terms.

Why you are not in a committed relationship with him

Your "guy" (we'll call him) has become **way** too comfortable with you. He knows you're into him and like a comfy couch or a favorite pair of pajamas he just slips you on when he wants. It's time for us to take a journey to enlighten you and fix this.

A man needs a challenge. It is inherent to us. Your goal is to create this challenge when you need to. Sitting around at his house in your sweats all day does not evoke a challenge to him. Staying aloof at times and upsetting the balance of power makes him **want** you to sit around all day in your sweats. Create this situation and he will commit!

Let's create this situation:

Step 1: Stop making him your hobby

Never make your guy your hobby. I realize you want to be with him all the time but you must re-route this emotion, at least temporarily. Remember that photography class you wanted to take? Take it! Keep your passions alive. Too many women give up their interests because of the man in their lives and they don't even realize it. He will become interested in you as soon as he realizes he's NOT the main focus in your life. Understand this; A man always needs to have a sense of "feeling free" even if he is married with 5 kids. A woman rarely provides this and instead places full-time demands on her man. Give him a break by pursuing your own hobbies and friends and watch what happens.

ACTION TO TAKE NOW:

Stop being needy and clingy. I realize we're all like this at times. Later you can do this, but NOT now. Now is the time to break this habit. Reestablish contact with your friends and start planning events WITHOUT him.

If you make him your hobby you will lose him, if you chase your dreams you will keep him.

Step 2: Become a woman of value

I teach my men readers this and it applies to you too. Don't let the men in your life dictate your self-esteem. Self-worth comes from within, and once you claim it you become a woman that is very attractive to others **including** men. Your time becomes valuable. This affects **who** you decide to share your time with. No longer does that couch potato of a boyfriend fit the bill. You automatically make upgrades to that man in your life. Compromise becomes less take and more give. Finding a man that complements your life becomes your focus.

> Women are always putting the cart before the horse. They feel they need to find a man first, and themselves later. Not so! Women need to find themselves first, which in turn leads to and attracts the proper guy.

So how do you become a woman of value? It's a gradual process, but it's one that can begin today. Find your passion and pursue it like a honey badger. It's this passion that will eventually give you lifelong happiness. Build upon it. Start to hang out with people that share the same love. Teach others about it. One of my passions is surfing. Life begins when I'm on my board. I like meeting and dating fellow female surfers. This will work for you too.

I dig deep into this subject in my new confidence-building book: *The Social Tigress*.

ACTIONS TO TAKE NOW:

Don't think you have any passions? Nonsense! Sit down right now and brainstorm. Write down anything that makes you happy. Then set up some goals to make these passions reality. Is it dance? Then tomorrow Google a dance class in your town and sign up.

Two positive things happen: you start to build self-esteem, and your guy starts to wonder what the hell you are doing! This step is an integral part of your transformation to get and hold onto the man of your dreams. If you're single, this pursuit will lead to a guy with similar interests, not some professional pick-up artist just trying to screw you on Saturday night.

Step 3: Establish a social life outside of his

Maybe you have a social life already but if you don't you **must** create one. Part of stopping him from becoming your hobby is creating a social network outside of his. This is the place where you will retreat and get his mind thinking about what you are doing and with whom you're doing it with.

If you have no other social life then Step #2 just gave you one. Also the fact that you **don't** have an outside social life becomes much more powerful when suddenly you create one in his eyes. Again he asks, "What the hell is she doing?" The seeds get planted that change is in the air and he better pay attention.

You will need your friends to sustain this relationship. You will understand this more in later chapters. Too many women go "all in" with a guy and ditch their friends. This chokes him, kills the challenge he needs and puts you at risk emotionally.

Your girlfriends and guy friends are going to be your escape when your man starts to go rogue.

> When a man starts to take you for granted I call this "going rogue".

You must keep a parallel social life in place. There will times when you need to get away from him to get him to *desire you again* and this social support system will be there for you.

Step 4: Kryptonite!

Now comes the fun part. Step #4 consists of three tactics.

You have developed a pattern with your guy. Tuesday nights you go over to his place and Saturday and Sundays you spend together. You bitch and whine about getting together more often. On occasion you fight about where your relationship is heading.

If this sounds familiar, then good—I've got the perfect solution for you. This three-step strategy will solve **all** of your issues with men. It flows through and connects this report in every chapter.

These three lethal steps will solve:

- Sexual issues
- Wandering eyes
- Intimacy issues
- Commitment
- Couch potatoes
- Lack of attention
- Lack of motivation
- Picking up that hot guy on Saturday night

Starting **today**, you need to make these three things happen:

- **React differently and break your routine**
- **Show signs of caring less**
- **Use the power of an affair**

#1 -React differently to him and break your routine

People are creatures of habit. We hit the same gym, coffee shop and mall. You have a girl's night out once a week, and you take roughly the same route to work every day. All in all, it's a life of routine that we rarely deviate from.

Let's move to personalities. We all have a basic set of traits. Yes sometimes we can be funny or crazy but we keep the same default set of characteristics with people we interact with. People label us. She is funny or crazy or adventurous. That guy over there is strange, funny and bold.

If you break your routine with your man you become mysterious to him and this shifts control to you. This is accomplished by establishing a pattern and then breaking it. He thinks he knows you, and then suddenly you react totally different. This will keep him magnetized towards you.

Remember the movie *Wedding Crashers*? Vince Vaughn has sex with Isla Fisher. She told Vince she was a virgin.

After hooking up on the beach Vince couldn't get away from her. She was needy and clingy. But something interesting happens; He finds out she was lying about being a virgin. Suddenly, Vince falls for her. Why? Everything Vince **thought** he knew about her changed when he realized that **he** got played.

Sure it's a movie, but this is **exactly** the stuff that I'm talking about. Always keep a carrot on a stick with a guy. Keep the challenge alive. This is the kryptonite I'm conveying to you.

Change the way you have sex. Do him on an elevator. Give him awesome sex for 2 days. Then spoon feed sex to him; "Sorry that's all you get until I decide I want to give you more."

Change how you text him. Change your fashion: miniskirt tonight, 60's chic tomorrow. Go out with your librarian look and let down your locks right in front of him.

Let him label you and change in motion. This drives a man mad! He can't be bored because every day he has a new box of chocolates.

This works when meeting men also. When I'm out with my guy friends perusing the females this; "I can't figure this girl out" is the #1 feature that attracts us to a woman other than initial looks. It works in relationships or simply meeting guys at the gym.

After hundreds of interviews guys tell me that women can infuse excitement back into their relationship if their girl would be mysterious at times...breaking their routine in as many ways as possible accomplishes this in spades.

This explains why a man is always seeking a girl that is **different** from you. If you become that multifaceted girl, guess what? He only needs **you**! I'm not saying change your personality! I'm asking you to make use of all the personalities inside you. Put your fantasies to work! The bonus is you get to explore him and yourself in a much deeper way. Trust me, a guy will be excited to explore with you!

Now don't go crazy with this—use this power measurably and when you need it, and back off upon success. If overused you could turn into a multi-personality Sybil.

This works like the **bomb** in relationships. For example; you are having sex once a week and it's becoming less and less frequent. He doesn't seem to care for you emotionally and he is taking you for granted. *He is going rogue.* Every day is the same routine, so **break it!** Don't even have sex that one night and watch what happens. Instead, take off with your friends (without any anger) for a weekend and be very vague about your plans.

If he gets angry, then **good**; this means he cares. React kindly and show more signs that you are not that into him (next step.) This starts my process of you gaining control and an eventual commitment.

> When a man goes rogue you are starting to lose him. He is bored with you. He has labeled you and the relationship starts its downward path. When you change even the simplest routine he pops out of his hole like a varmint in *Caddyshack*.

#2- Show Signs of Caring Less

When you begin to act differently toward him and break your routine at the same time you convey an attitude that tells him you are not that into him anymore. This is accomplished by spending more time with your friends and the step above. Make sure this is done happily and with **no** anger on your part. This way he truly starts to think that he is losing you (potentially to some other man.)

This is a **very** powerful step. Men are very competitive creatures and we fight for what we consider to be ours. This characteristic is embedded deep within our DNA. Once we have something or someone we tend to take it (you) for granted and we move onto the next challenge. When you break bad it forces us to reconsider just how valuable you are. Our minds start to process all the good that you have brought into our lives. But it takes this trigger for us to see the forest for the trees.

This is a completely innate idea to a man, and you may not see or understand the entire picture of what I'm saying. But you **can** use this to get whatever you want. The important thing is when he awakens and shows desire again, be prepared to show him the new you and not the same you who made him your hobby and was not a woman of value.

This leads to the next step...

#3- The Power of the Possibility of an Affair

Believe it or not, but sometimes an affair is the last resort and is the **most** powerful final ultimatum in my tactical toolbox. You don't necessarily have to have a fling just put the potential in his head. Oftentimes the mere thought that you are having an affair will change a man in a heartbeat. This digs deep into fantasies that men have about threesomes and having a guy inside of you. This stirs incredible emotion in a man and triggers his desire to get you back!

GOING NUCLEAR

As your final resort, go out with another guy. This, of course, is not to be taken lightly. This step is **so** powerful that some men will snap at you or the other guy. **Do not** tell him directly, and **do not** have an affair with one of his friends. And if the guy you're with is hotheaded, stay away from this altogether (and then ditch him for good measure.

Why would you want an angry dude in the first place?)

Make his imagination run wild, maybe by posting a pic with a bunch of your girlfriends and "the other guy" on Facebook. If he has one ounce of love for you he will **try** to rein you in instantly. He will change his ways. This is the magic and this is your ultimate kryptonite to be used sparingly and as a last resort.

SOME IMPORTANT POINTS

- All men will react to these measures; it's just a matter to what degree. This, in turn, will determine how far you must go. It might be as simple as you spending one night a week out with your friends or as far as an affair...either way he will be "all in" if done measurable.

- You must control your emotions. Don't bitch. Don't whine. Go out with your girlfriends, like you never have, but be very polite about it. If you storm out of the house it doesn't work because he will say, "thank God the bitch is gone."

- For you single women out there, this works too. The key is to meet a guy at a social venue and establish a pattern. This can be accomplished with fashion and your personality. Guys are simple and we go right to our stupid labels. You have tattoos, we think you're a bad girl that wants a bad boy. You have 6-inch pumps and we think you're easy.

- Meet us, establish a trend and shift it. Act tough and turn innocent. Act conservative, dress conservative and dance like crazy. We love this shit. We want to run over and ask you out! The reality is women dress conservative and they act conservative. They are easy to label and it bores us. Girls just won't make the shift.

- This tactic is especially helpful for girls that are less than attractive. This can level the field as your personality will become magnetic to men.

Step #5: You're the New Sheriff in Town

You'll take the steps above as far as you need to and do them as often as you have to. Your man will now show signs of **desire** again. He will be less likely to blow you off for a guy's night out for fear you will be doing the same to him. In fact every time he's not with you he'll be thinking about you and who you're with. You've "planted the seed" that you are a confident, beautiful woman and he is fucking lucky to be with you.

If for some reason he hasn't come around then you need to step it up. Do this: make like you are ready to hit him with another "relationship talk," but instead of saying the usual, ("I want a ring on my finger by July!"), instead say, "I'm going to spend more time with my friends, so let's not do Friday nights anymore."

Wow! You just kicked him in the chops. Follow through with this tactic and he will ask to spend more time with you!

Consider the human and cat relationship:

Show too much attention to our furry friend and he will walk away. Ignore puss in boots and he will be all over you!

At this stage you will be able to **advance** your relationship further. Let him talk and then introduce new ground rules like it was his idea all along. No ultimatums, just some new ground rules. Make the rules geared towards you and him, but (and this is important) include time spent with **your** friends. This confuses him and increases his desire.

Do NOT fall back into the same relationship for any length of time.

This is where you need to judge your man. Some women have found that doing my strategies just once scares the man fetal and she can go back to how things were. Other girls find that their man needs to be toilet trained on a constant weekly or monthly schedule. In almost all cases the man comes around and needs a dog biscuit less and less.

Kryptonite works like the bomb and your friends are the fuse. Remember why I said your friends are the key to this working? They are the social network that will keep your man from going rogue—USE IT!

THE RESULTS
OF YOUR ACTIONS

You have gained your man back, but you've also achieved something else: your self-esteem.

What you will find is a new sense of confidence as the power shifts over to you. What you need to do is **feed** off this! Empower yourself! You might see an unflattering man in front of you. He is not used to having to pursue you and you are not used to him acting this way. This is how men react when we realize that we could lose our partner.

Warning: Don't be surprised if you suddenly realize that you can do BETTER than this guy you are currently with. Women have told me this quite often. Confidence and control triggers thoughts of upgrading. Suddenly you may find this guy compromises your life instead of complementing it.

Take this Kryptonite and use it whenever your guy goes rogue. The very thought of you exercising this power will make him change his ways going forward.

This concept explains why we get so excited about new relationships. It's all about the mystery. After dating or being married for a while, rogue will eventually set in. At this critical juncture you **must** reintroduce the excitement by implementing my five steps above.

So what just happened? He **desires** you again. And when your guy desires you, bad habits die. Suddenly he gets his ass to the gym, he stops farting and belching all the time, the toilet seat gets put down and the romance comes back.

Accomplish these five steps before he ever goes rogue and you will never need my advice again!

Get it? Good! Now it's time to put it to work for you. Don't let your girlfriends talk you out of this...**they are not men, and don't know how important these rules are.**

NOTE: The ONLY time this has failed is when a couple has let things go too far. They might already be seeing someone else they really like or they have said too many hurtful things to each other. This means you have a serious problem. I would consider getting out of the relationship as there are too many better choices for you.

KRYPTONITE IN ACTION

In this chapter we are going take our steps and insert them into a common relationship problem.

PROBLEM: He wants to be with his friends and not you

Women need to change how they direct their emotions towards men. You can't come after us, this doesn't work. In fact, you will get the direct opposite result you are seeking.

Stop Your Bitching Today

Women envy the relationships that men have with their buddies. I hear the following line (or some version) all the time:

"If you spent as much time with me as you do your football buddies I wouldn't complain."

The result? The guy spends **more** time with his football buddies and then heaps on massive amounts of extra contempt for **you**. You may get him to stay at home (or be with you if you don't live together) but he won't be enjoying you because the contempt is building. Even if you are real nice to him it doesn't matter the damage has been done.

The Solution

Instead, let him go see his friends. Then go see **your** girlfriends. "Hmmm," you say, "sounds counterproductive." Ah but by doing this you just created the shift. Kryptonite kicks in again. He is used to you bitching about him leaving. But with this method you catch him off guard with an "Okay, I'll go meet my friends."

The key is to not get angry (or at least to hide it). Storming out of the house will not work. That puts him on a guilt trip and we don't want that.

> You don't want guilt from him, you want DESIRE.

As soon as you happily say, "I'll go see my friends" watch his reaction. He will be confused. He will wonder why you have changed. He will think you are having an affair or aren't into him as much anymore...SNAP! You just gained control.

Go see your girls. The first thing you will notice is he will be texting you more to "check in." Don't respond. Or even better: respond but be very nice and say, "I gotta go babe."

Your goal is to get his simple mind thinking that other single guys might be around you. Guys check on their girls to make sure they are still at their beck and call. By not responding, his great time with his friends (and other girls in some cases) disappears. **Now** he would rather be with **you**.

This is how the game is played and this is how you will **always** win. Game him until he **wants** to be with you.

YOU HOLD ALL THE CARDS!

Points to remember:

- Never bitch
- He wants to see his friends, go see yours (happily). Game on!
- Don't respond
- Create a vibe of a possible affair
- Stay nice but be a bit aloof
- Continue until his desire builds for you

BONUS TRAINING:

TEACH HIM TO ROLL OVER AND SIT

Is He a Keeper? My 3 Steps

The scenario: You met a guy last week and a couple dates later you like him. How do you know for sure that he is a decent guy?

WHAT YOU DO

Women view men like a horse through blinders. They see only the good. You give guys the benefit of the doubt **way** too often. You often sleep with them too soon. This is especially troubling as great sex clouds your mind even more. Your friends hint at the red flags and all you see is the twinkle in his eyes. I can't review my own Kindle eBook and you can't review your own man. You need a way to step back and look at his true worth.

THE SOLUTION

1) Get him drunk. Yeah, I know this sounds lame but you need to. Oh, **you** need to stay somewhat sober for obvious reasons or this step will fail. Alcohol is a truth serum to men. Think crystal ball and palm reading as he lies face down in a dumpster. So much can be gained. You will learn how much he drinks and if he is an alcoholic. You will learn if he is an obnoxious drunk; this will mean you will be defending him in fights. Does he hit on women? Does he hit on men? Does he hit on horses? Does he juggle or drop kick cats? Does he drive drunk? Stupid fast? Sex: can he perform? What does he say? Oh, the skeletons that can be unearthed in the presence of a six pack and patron shots. Who knew alcohol had so many practical uses?!

2) Have your friends meet him. Set up an informal get together so Mr. Stud can meet and greet the peeps. This is huge. You have blinders on but your girls see the **real** picture! Your friends will give you an unbiased review. **Listen** to them. Don't be the zillionth girl who said, "I should have listened to you."

3) Meet his friends. The biggest of all! Don't just meet his friends see how he acts when you say you want to meet his friends (body language). He should be happy about this. Does he have friends? Once in the group answer these questions about him:

- Is he respected?
- Is he the alpha?
- If not, where is he in the group?
- Does he become shy? Beta.
- How does he treat you?
- Does his personality change? If so, how?
- What are his friends like? Single? Girl chasers?
- Does he try to impress you?
- Did any lies come out?

LEVEL 1 RED FLAGS (RUN!)

Pay particular attention to his personality. If he changes and becomes part of the guy group then you need to be careful of what I call a "guys guy." If he is already siding with his friends he will ALWAYS put them ahead of you. This is a red flag. If all his friends are players—**he is too!** If you find he outright lied to you, then lose this guy NOW.

LEVEL 2 (YOU CAN WORK WITH THIS)

If he tries to impress you too much, this is a sign of low esteem. This could be the symbolism of a clingy or a needy man. If his friends crap on him, then he is a beta male—one that **you** most certainly will be dominating. These are smaller items; ones that some women can deal with...you need to decide.

LEVEL 3 (WHERE'S MY BIRTH PROTECTION!)

If his friends exposed some "exaggerations", I would not be too concerned. I think we all enhance our lives a little when we meet someone for the first time. Also, every guy will change a little bit when they combine their two worlds, so don't get too freaked about this. I want you to look for a major change as this means he was manipulating his personality when you first met.

Now I don't know you so I don't know the type of guy you like. I do know you deserve the best and every woman deserves at least the basics; respect of your body, trust, and emotional support. My favorite part is to go out with women and help them meet guys. I then know you, and I can read the guys you run into. This gets **real** fun as you might imagine.

Back to meeting his friends. Your new guy should treat you with total respect. He should realize that you do not know anyone and help you merge with his friends. He should be overly attentive and, ideally, chivalrous. He should be relaxed. If one of his friends gets out of line he should come to your defense.

This is the one time when clingy can be OK until you give the all clear signal. This guy could be a great catch!

———————————————

I'm Done Playing Games

Women tell me this all the time, especially older women. The bottom line is games need to be played in every relationship. There is no white picket fence unless you build one. Things will go wrong on each side. Getting bored, limited sex or no sex at all, couch potatoes and adultery will happen if **you** don't step in. Divorce is so common because people don't know how to react to these situations.

> I am giving you the tools, the wood for the pickets and the white paint you need to build that fence!

THE GOOD NEWS

You'll only have to play games a very small percentage of the time. The beauty is once played the guy will know what you are capable of and just the thought of you using your Kryptonite will make him think twice!

_____

We Are Simple Creatures, Treat Us So

Women are complicated, I get that. We are simple. Communicate to us in simple terms, dumb it down. I am not talking about IQ. You could be dating a scientist or a doctor, it doesn't matter.

WHAT YOU DO

You come home upset and hit us with ten different things that went wrong with your day. Somewhere in this War and Peace novel is the fact that you are upset about something **specific** that happened at work. So tell us at the very start!

We can't figure it out and you expect us to. You are already upset, now you are even more upset that we can't mind read what the hell went wrong with your day. Next, we try to solve the problem. "Honey, why don't you look for another job?" Now you want to **kill** us. You **don't** want the problem solved you want us to **listen** to you.

I tell my guy readers; "Don't try to solve the problem. Instead, listen to her."

THE SOLUTION

"Ok, I'm listening, but how are we expected to change what comes naturally to us as women?"

My solution is this: I understand that you need to vent about your day but don't vent that way to us. Instead, on your way home let loose to your girlfriend. She understands you and she will listen and will not try to solve the problem. This way you are a little calmer when you speak to us. Now dumb things down and tell us exactly why you are upset and we will listen. Treat us like the simple creatures we are.

Your Timing Sucks, Learn When to Talk to a Man

Let's talk about communication and timing. I understand how much you need to communicate. We are apes, we like to smash things and communicate that way. We will talk but timing is everything.

WHAT YOU DO

Many women want to talk after sex. This is a warm and fuzzy time for you. You have bonded with your special guy. This is quite natural to want to talk about tomorrow's plans or where you are headed in the relationship.

Unfortunately, this is poison to a guy. Things happen inside a man's body after sex that just shut us down. We **need** to relax. We want to sleep. We can't communicate. Next, you take this personally like we don't like/love you anymore and the downward spiral begins. Long term we may even avoid sex because we know "the talk" is coming.

Also, right after work is a bad time to talk. Let's say we are meeting for a drink Tuesday after work or college classes. We will show up with a smile, but we are stressed. You will not know as we don't display our emotions. We are not ready for anything heavy.

THE SOLUTION

Talk to us when we are happy. The time to connect with us is when we are on a high together, when we are laughing mutually and really getting along.

Talk to us **before** sex. Yes, I said it. We want you and we are horny and you are in total control...**use** it. Keep the tone light. I didn't say the subject matter, I said the tone. Smile when you are asking questions and you will be amazed at the stuff you can get from us. Tease the hell out of us and we will take you to dinner, the opera or get you that 600th pair of shoes that you want.

After sex, I need you to act like a guy. Control your emotions and if you can't, go call your girlfriend. The result? Again, back to your Kryptonite: you have changed your pattern and the man will take notice and become more interested. His mind thinks you might be a little less interested in him and he will try harder and communicate better.

Picture this: You just had great sex. Your guy is waiting for the "cuddling and talking" time to come, which he hates. Instead, you get up and say, "I'm meeting Jess for lunch, see ya later."

This is powerful stuff! Don't try to understand it, that's for psychologist, just do it and enjoy the results!

This Is Your New Bar Etiquette

I have a great chapter covering the bar scene in detail in my new book, *The Social Tigress*, that you need to read... you'll love it!

Ok, we have moved to the bar/club. First, I want to define the bar scene.

You are swimming with the sharks. The guy you want to meet is **not** in the room. Let me qualify that. He might be there but he will **rarely**, if ever, approach you. Now there are exceptions to everything, of course. Obviously, if you are out just to get laid and you want an alpha man, then cool...I get that. But for many of you, your goal is to hunt down dating material.

PUAs (pick up artists) are good. They will have checked you out long before you have seen them. They will have studied your body language and what type of person you are. They will even change their personality types to fit you. Yes, it's almost scary.

They will approach with humor, looks and maybe props to impress you and your girlfriends. They are out for one thing and you know what it is. They are players and you will NOT convert them (again, exceptions, but this would take some serious doing.)

WHAT YOU DO

Women believe this guy is for real. They go for this jerk and they sleep with him. As soon as this happens, they're toast. These men are misogynists. The cycle begins. You are hurt and taking it completely personal as you do. You blame yourself for doing something wrong. This guy will have you believing that. You may even see him again and he won't even acknowledge you unless he is drunk, and he hasn't succeeded with another mark. Another chink in your self-esteem gets imprinted.

THE SOLUTION

You are better than this. Don't ever let a guy play you. If you become a woman of value, this man is like a wounded mouse around a cat. He is pitiful and unworthy.

Women ask me this question all the time, "Why can't I find a decent guy?" My question back is always: "What does your social life consist of, where do you go?" Amazingly, I get the same answer: "Here."

Treat bars as what they are: pick up spots. Enjoy yourself, your friends and the music, but forget about your knight in shinning armor. Instead, think about STDs in the morning.

Play with guys. Go along with their game, get them aroused and then trash them. If they have a quiet friend, then give him all the attention. Or, ignore the stiffs. If you have to engage, then look around and find a man that is not in the forefront and make serious eye contact or, better yet, approach him. Yes, I said it. We do not think you're a slut if you approach us. In fact, it takes all the pressure off and we can act like ourselves.

Change your social life. Follow your passions and hobbies. Go whitewater rafting or on a ski trip with some friends or alone. When you least expect it, this is where you will meet a decent man.

The Power of Aloof

Many principles I teach men apply to women as well. Staying aloof is one of them. This usually goes against what you want to do and that is to communicate with us when things are spiraling down.

Again, you must control your emotions temporarily. By going aloof a man thinks you are now the one losing interest and this is critical. You become mysterious. A guy naturally starts to think you are seeing someone else. This triggers change.

WHAT YOU DO

If you are in a casual relationship or just meeting a man you make yourself too available. This kills the challenge and sets him up as your hobby. You may hang out at his house for days on end and become a couch potato. Or you may cater to the man by doing his laundry and paying his bills. This is nurturing stuff like his mom may do. Soon you take over all his drawers with tampons and lingerie.

THE SOLUTION

Don't be available when he needs you. Get together on your time. Make him wait. Spoon feed him sex. Don't show your hand until he shows you his. Never get into the nurturing mode unless he has truly committed to you. You are not his mother and he hasn't shown you anything that tells you that **your** time is worth spending with him. Keep this attitude and you will hold **all** the cards. This will make him realize how much of a *woman of value* you really are.

The Pendulum Effect

Here's the scenario. You just broke up with your "party animal" boyfriend. He had his bright moments, of course. He was great in the sack, flamboyant, and had a terrific sense of humor. Then he cheated on you. What do you do? You go out and find the same type of guy and, before you know it, you're single again.

Sound familiar? Well, if it makes you feel any better, guys do the same thing, just not on the same level. We tend to take more time off in between relationships, too.

WHAT YOU DO

After the 5th break-up with the same type guy, women will go for the polar opposite of what they were dating. What happens? The same thing. But this time, Harold the dweeb with the plaid shirt got his ass dumped by you because you were bored out of your mind and (big surprise) Mr. Dweeb couldn't tell your butt hole from your clitoris.

I call this the pendulum effect. Women go for personalities that they shouldn't be going for. Then they swing the pendulum way too far the other way to counter their last man.

THE SOLUTION

Take a deep breath. Take some time off in between relationships. No, really. You talk about it, but you don't do it. I know because I have run into quite a few girls telling me they can't go home with me because they just got out of relationship. Next day, I'm getting asked how I like my eggs.

People are needy so they count on their self-esteem to be created by the relationship. This is wrong. Confidence is only gained from within. You **know** these facts but they need to be repeated. This book is not about your inner game but you will gain self-esteem by default when you learn how to control the men in your lives.

———————————————————

The Drive to the Hoop

I would be a fool not to mention sex. This is not a sex book so I will keep things geared towards gaming men.

Guys don't want you to know how much power that body of yours has! Ironically, with all the muscles, alpha crap and dominance a man can bestow on a woman there is **nothing** that compares to the power of the pussy.

> ### The power of your pussy can stop us in our tracks.

And yet you don't use it wisely most of the time. I understand that some women just want to go out and get laid. Again, I get that and this chapter will not apply to you.

Q: Should I sleep with a guy on a first date?

A: No, no, and no again. Why would you? If you sleep with me on the first date then I will **not** think of you as a future girlfriend or, dare I say, wife. That said I will still **try** to get you in the sack. This is almost a shit test to see if you will. If you say yes, then lucky me I'm getting laid but unlucky me I'm still searching for the girl of my dreams.

Don't demean yourself, tease the guy and get out of there. If he doesn't call, then you just proved all he wanted was sex. If he does call, great, this is a sign of a keeper.

Q: When should I have sex?

A: The answer is when it's time. Have you followed my advice above? Have you met his friends? Have you witnessed him drunk? Has he met your friends? Did he pass these tests? Have you done a background test on him? These are the mere basics. **Now** listen to your heart. If women just did these obvious steps, they would save themselves a world of emotional hardship.

Future Sex

If you please your guy, he will never stray. Think a loyal dog. Feed him average canned food and he might go to the neighbor's house. Feed him filet and he's staying home! Sex is the same.

Here's the "filet" I'm talking about:

Change your sexual ways often. Keep him begging by being mysterious. Spoon feed him sex and other times give it to him in massive doses. Don't make every session about you. Guys complain that women come with "manuals", that it takes 3 chimpanzees and an albino midget to get his girl off.

Communicate about sex and at the **proper** time. Tell each other what the other one likes. Make it fun and into a "show and tell" process. **Never** tell a guy he's doing it wrong! Instead say, "that feels good, now higher." At first you almost have to lie to the guy that he is good in bed even if he sucks. Only then can you direct him towards greatness.

Remember this is a very sensitive area for men. We all think we are great in bed. Inside we know we need direction as all women are different. Give us that direction in a very positive way.

The Justice Trap

Women complain when orgasms aren't evenly distributed. The reality is we get off so easy that the score will **never** be even. If you accept that fact, then you will be getting off much more often too because we will be content and want you to be the same. When the pressure of you having an orgasm always looms, guess what? We avoid it and hit the porn site.

Keep It Crazy

Get out of the bedroom and into elevators! Do things like the mile high club, role playing, buy restraints and toys and a guy will always remember and want more. Don't fall into a rut. Experiment before we cum not after!

Lose the Porn

Porn is a bad thing. It dulls and desensitizes people. I know guys that can't even have a relationship because they watch so much porn. If you are keeping things crazy under the sheets (and in the car), your man will never need porn. You will and should be his porn star and he yours. Feel free to watch porn together to get new ideas - that's totally okay.

SPECIAL BONUS:

BECOME THE LOVE OF HIS LIFE

Congratulations! You've done your due diligence above and he's back. Now let's step away from the games and get back to your relationship.

For making it this far, I wanted to award you ladies with a few final thoughts that I think are absolutely essential to any long lasting relationship. Take these tips and run with them—if you follow through with them, he will give you the life you've always wanted.

Be His Prize

Remember going to the fair as a kid and hoping to win the elusive furry prize that sat on the top shelf? You had to have it but never (at least I never!) got the damn thing.

Become his top shelf prize.

Make him want you and only you for the rest of his life. How? Ah, glad you asked. As you may know I own a top dating advice site for men and I asked this question to thousands of men.

A **surprising** answer rose to the top: *ENTER HIS WORLD*

Sounds obvious right? But the fact is that most women don't. Sure they might live with this man or even be married with kids but do they really enter into their significant others world?

My relationship flourishes today because my girlfriend and I are a team. She actively participates when I wash the car, fix things around the house or even mow the lawn. Everyday mundane chores are fun. When she grocery shops, I'll often show up with another cart and race her around the store with the goal of never stopping the cart. These things sound silly and stupid but they are the fabric that keeps a guy loving you.

HERE'S WHY

Couples that beat the odds are a **team**. They have become a team because they have both chosen to share common interests. If you love someone then you love their interests, too. They are the ones that, well, make most of us puke because they get along so well. They are inseparable. Like dropping off an infant at daycare for the first time this team misses the other almost instantly. They always have each other's backs both in private and in public. A man **needs** this to fall in love, to feel validated that he is desirable, unique and very special compared to all others.

To want to participate in your man's passions doesn't mean you suck up to him or even agree with everything he says or does. It means you need to enter his world on every level. Successful couples complement each other and support each other through life without ever undermining the other. This means you accept with open arms his hobbies and passions.

HERE'S HOW

Make an effort to understand what he really likes and why. Is it sports? Hang gliding? Cooking? Does he love the mountains? Can he build things out of wood? Or is he into German Shepard's? Ask him to teach you his hobbies and research these passions on your own. Many women go through their relationships without this key ingredient... the intertwining of hobbies with their significant other. Don't just go shopping when he is working on his Ford Mustang—help him!

You might actually enjoy what he does. Just because he makes furniture and you know nothing about it doesn't mean that you wouldn't love to do it. Try it. Think of what you could gain: more time spent with the man you crave and a new hobby to enlighten your life. What could be better?

Not only will you see results but he will be impressed that you **care**. This is a **huge** trait that men file into their "she could be a keeper" bin—a woman that actually wants to participate in something that he is totally passionate about. Wow!

Watch Him Reciprocate

As a bonus play, you might very well find your man asking and wanting to know and participate in **your** interests. Look for this, but don't demand it. If he does, then guess what? **You** just found yourself a keeper.

A reader friend told me that his girlfriend was into this conservation program. Once a month she visited all the different streams and tributaries in her area and recorded various plant and animal life. What did he do? Without being asked, he went with her and met some new friends and eventually got very active alongside his girlfriend.

What usually happens? I think you know the answer. You go shopping with your girlfriends while your guy watches football or works on his motorcycle and loneliness and maybe contempt start to seed the relationship. Instead, you could be with this guy when he is doing what he loves and guess what? He will equate you with this love. Yes, it's psychology at work.

I know, you say you have no interest in football and motorcycles. How would you ever know? We say that we have zero interest in your veterinarian studies or your yoga class. How would we know? Stop the sexist standoff and be the first to enter his world. He has many passions (or he should) so pick one and jump in!

In Summary

Get involved with his day, his mundane chores, his work and hobbies. If he resists, dump his ass because he's not worth it. If he opens up to you, then jump in. Next, see if he reciprocates. Ask him to. If he doesn't, then you need to decide if he is still worth your time.

If he does these 2 things, then you have yourself a keeper and I bow to you!

Try this one amazing tip. Enter his world and BECOME HIS PRIZE and watch the possibilities rise up before you.

FINDING
THE 5 STEPS
DIFFICULT?

READ THIS EMAIL!

I want to thank the thousands of ladies that have read my book! I have been getting a lot of women emailing me with their questions and success stories and I love it! I've had some women that are trying hard (and I commend them) but have gotten stuck on an issue concerning following through.

This email in particular was perfect to address and solve this concern.

Camilla wrote:

Hi Gregg -

I just finished reading your e-book "Who Holds The Cards Now?" and I have work to do with my lazy/ comfortable boyfriend. He's gotten comfortable and bored with me, I've always made him a priority

- been too available and too responsive at times. Since reading your book I've changed the way I text him in that I take my sweet ass time getting back to him (much like he does to me), sometimes it's a short wait and other times I take hours upon hours. I also changed my responses to him to be shorter and less "deep" -- I've been keeping it light and breezy. What seems to be happening is he's being even LESS responsive than before. I don't see a new found eagerness for him to spend time or communicate. He doesn't seem worried at all. This weekend he'll probably want to spend time, I've never turned him down (my fault), I think this weekend I'm going to say something like "I'd love to but I have other plans, maybe we can catch up next weekend?" -- is that good? I feel a sense of empowerment during this process, but at times I also have overwhelming feelings of nervousness and anxiety that he might just take my new approach as a lack of interest and leave me alone all together. I'm a little scared, even though still planning to follow through. Do you think I just need to give this new approach more time to see results? Thanks so much for all your advice and help....

Camilla and others have put my tactics to work on a **small scale** and seen their significant others not react or react negatively. This makes them back off and nothing gets resolved.

Ladies you need to FOLLOW through on a **large and consistent scale.** If you just change a few little things then the guy will probably just get annoyed with you. Change major things and do it with urgency. I understand this is scary and this probably goes against everything that you WANT to do-but you need to trust the system...it works. Like I said, we can train HIM; it's you that may lack the confidence to follow through.

Camilla is concerned that she will lose him in the above email. I understand her concern but what does she have to lose? She is unhappy now and at this rate she will lose him anyway. At the very least their relationship will suck for a very long time to come.

This is my response to Camilla:

Hi Camilla.

You have dipped your toes into the male psyche swimming pool and I commend your efforts so far. You are nervous...this is very common. You haven't gotten the desired response from your man because you haven't followed through. You're probably just annoying him so he is reacting the way he is. He doesn't believe for a second that you have any power or can dictate the terms in this relationship.

This makes you even more POWERFUL!

You need to show him that YOU are losing interest

in HIM. I know you are not but he has gotten complacent- let's face it. I love your idea of saying, "I'd love to but I have other plans, maybe we can catch up next weekend?" THIS is the way to go. THIS will get him thinking something is wrong. THIS will bring change. DON'T make him your hobby or priority!

Also, use the power of your body. Change your sex patterns with him. Shut him off when you normally would have sex. Spoon feed him sex when YOU want to. And do some crazier stuff in the bedroom than normal if you have it in you. Basically, change as much of your game as you can with him and treat him like he treats YOU. Yes, hide those female emotions for a bit until he comes back to you.

As far as being scared; I understand your concern but ask yourself this; Are you happy with the way things are? Are things getting better? Or worse? If you continue I think there is a strong possibility that you will be breaking up anyway. If you believe this, then what do you have to lose?

Create a social network outside of his, and use it. Show him that you have options and that your time is valuable. If you blow him off for the first time and he breaks up - did he really even love you in the first place?

Hope this helps,

Gregg

In summary, your man is seeing a side of you that he hasn't witnessed before. He doesn't know how to react. So expect the unexpected and don't get worried if he responds to you negatively at first. Many men try to "play it cool." They lie to themselves and think, "F*** her if she wants to be with her friends tonight, I don't care."

The reality is he DOES care and he is hurt. A few more salvos from you and suddenly he is going to have to care (if he loves you) and he will turn positive towards you. Guys have a huge self ego and you are knocking it down briefly so expect some rebellion, especially out of an alpha. Think poker; you have a pair of ACES (your body, mind and pure awesomeness) and he has squat. Make him realize what he is going up against and he will fold!!

Keep the questions rolling.

Carry on, my crazy Fembotts!

A BIT ABOUT

YOUR DRILL SARGEANT

So as I'm sure you ladies know by now, my name is Gregg. And what you've probably guessed at over the course of this book is that I've had a lot of time to be single and, yes, to enjoy it! Now, that doesn't mean that I haven't taken a walk down relationship road once or twice. It's just that for me, being single is the state of mind that I find most agreeable for now.

If you ever get a chance to meet me, you'll quickly find that I'm a pretty friendly and generous (maybe too generous!) guy. In fact, I'm often showing that very same generosity by letting my friends stay at my place when their relationships take turns for the worst. While a buddy of mine is recovering, we tend to have a little fun, you know, to take his mind off things. We pal around for a few months, but soon enough my friends find other cuties that are worth settling down for.

This scenario happens quite a bit, enough times at least for my buddy Keith to tell me "Gregg, you've helped out so many of us at one point or another. Why don't you start a dating site?" Two years ago, I took him up on that advice, and my website KeysToSeductions.com was born. Its success has been amazing, and today I have over a hundred pages of content and 1000 unique visitors every day.

Why is the site so successful? I think it has something to do with me being a true natural when it comes to meeting and talking to women. I'm not sure how I hit on that particular skill. It may have been luck. Or you could chalk it up to the fact that I had three older sisters that tortured me when I was a little runt. I didn't have much interest in reading dating books, and when I finally got around to them I found that they were written poorly and offered little to no engagement. I knew I could do better.

The goal of KeysToSeductions, by the way, was to help men build their confidence enough to really get out there and start finding women of value. In a way, the advice I give to both men and women has more similarities than differences. Confidence and self-worth are critical, which is why this particular book focused so much on you, and not always the man in your life.

For the average guy that I write to at least, this is exactly what they need: confidence. Hell, I'm an average guy! I'm average height and average looking—and yet I love going up against Mr. Tall, Dark and Handsome and winning! I taught myself how to dance and that, along with making women laugh, is my social edge.

As for why I'm writing to women...the truth is that it was a natural next step. Being completely sincere here: I love and respect women, I honestly do. I have no interest in manipulating them, nor would I ever need to. Over the years, I've listened to what women have to say. I know them inside and out. I've been doing the dating coach thing and the single thing for so long now that it's safe to say I understand what gets under your skin, and what the biggest problems are with your dating lives.

No, I haven't dated the hottest supermodels alive and no, I haven't been from one TV show to the next promoting myself and my skillset in this regard. For the most part I'm quite private, and I like it like that. Still, my coaching takes me everywhere, from California to Nevada to Florida. It's a life I love to lead; and even though I often end up missing home (I grew up in Boston, and today I have homes in West Palm and Las Vegas) it's still the only life I can imagine leading.

MORE BOOKS

BY GREGG MICHAELSEN

For Women

The Social Tigress:
Dating Advice for Women to Attract Men and Get a Boyfriend

Power Texting Men!
The Best Texting Attraction Book to Get the Guy

For Men

From Zero to Hero:
A Modern Guys Guide to Understanding a Womans Heart
(with Kat Kingston)

Hook, Line & Date Her:
The Average Guy's Book to Attract, Meet and Date Quality Women

The Building of a Confident Man:
How to Create Self Esteem and Become More Attractive to Women

Find them on Amazon today!

Printed in Great Britain
by Amazon